Night Full of Diamonds

Jake St. John

Whiskey City Press
Copyright ©2021

for Jenn,
my partner in life and adventure

Table of Contents

How To Write A Poem

I'll start my poem
with words
penned
down your neck
I'll personify
the crook
and tell you
it holds
the most
beautiful words
I'll write my lines
across your hips
I'll leave
full stanzas
on your lips
a break
between
couplets
at your breasts
to emphasize
the beauty
of each letter
I leave
upon your skin
and when
the final words
have been
kissed
we'll lay

wrapped
in similes
and metaphors
and sheets
that cling
to us
like damp pages.

Wild

Moonlit nights
of starlit
oceans
nearing the
dawn
of lonely
gods.

Night Is The Hardest

Night is the hardest
when loneliness
rides in on a road
paved in moonlight
arriving with a bottle
and a trunk
full of thoughts
pouring glasses
full of solitude
everything appears
farther away
in the silence
of dim hours

people
and the safety net
of morning
seem out of reach
when you need them
most of all
standing
under the stars
bearing
the strain
of survival
you realize
it's just you
alone
in the fog.

Upon Waking

Morning fades
into the forest

the wind
shakes the sun

it falls
from trees

birds continue
to sing

the dog sleeps
in the yard

I awaken
the fire

my coffee
is strong

and opens my eyes.

Afternoon Hike

The dirt roads
that crisscross
my heart
are dusty
with memories

they meander
slowly
twisting
and turning
curving up
to the peak
of my soul

taking in
the views
of yesterday
that have
all been lost
to the wind

a forest
of thoughts
line my steps

making
my way
through
the years

under
the sun

a dead tree
cracks
and falls across
the route
all progress
forward
halted.

Vernal Equinox

The moon
spotlights
my loneliness
and lights up
the sound

even the stars
are dimmed
by her brilliance

standing
in silence
transfixed
by a night
that vibrates

thoughts
crowding
the shadows
that dance
around
the yard

eyes full
of stardust
a heart full
of promise
I open my arms
and hug the dawn.

Campsite Reveries

Dawn
smudges
light
through trees

you
uncoiling
night
with a smile
illuminating
my vitality

a wilderness
painted
in cosmic hues
I am
entwined
in the
laughter
of your
eyes

bathed
in sunlight
beneath
an azure sea
speckled
with the
remnants
of dreams
the day
spilling out
across a canvas
of skin.

Unsettled Peace

Loneliness
is good company
if I can keep
the thoughts at bay

but sometimes
they join a pack
and yip and howl
at the moon

like the coyotes
prowling under
the trees
on the far side
of the stonewall

and the fire mainly
keeps to itself
as it reduces
the night to ash

and standing here
in the shadow
of blossoming flames
I don't know

if I'm watching it
or it's watching me.

The Grim Reaper Is My Best Friend

The grim reaper
is my best friend
he walks
with me
everyday

sometimes
down the sidewalk
and into work
sometimes
into the woods
alone
we'll go

we sit
and talk
philosophy
and books
his favorite
author
is a prick
and mine
is a fraud

I don't
stop for lunch
but he'll pause
and eat
a ham sandwich

he is
kind enough
to pour me
a drink
at any time
of day

and
in the morning
we drink
black coffee
together
while laughing
at the news.

A Forest Of Thought

The tree
has no
political
allegiance
but stands
strong
and rooted
firm
not for beliefs
but for life.

In Your Absence

I spend my minutes
looking towards
the moon

a waning crescent
a sliver
in the night

you there
in the north woods
and me
here in the hills
of my birth

I think of you
below maritime stars
eyes lit
like a field
of mayflowers

I stand
by my pit
of fire

flames
kissing
the night
as I would
your neck

my heart
in your hands

one defends
and the other
conquers

you have
conquered
all of me

I lay myself
down before you
like a vast
tilled field
ready
to be sown

you have
dug your fingers
into the meadows
of my heart

you've planted
your seeds

come fall
we'll harvest grain.

Fireside

Flame and smoke
leave charred wood
rising wild in wind
of late summer day

there are no friends
here with me
yet the voice
from the TV
in the shack
speaks of sickness

birds still sing
somewhere
in the fading green
current of leaves

loneliness
should not be confused
with sadness
though they sprout
from the same garden

the trail of clouds
worn down by eyes
leads to the forest of night.

Solitary

I feel like Jack
on the peak
there is no
awakening
just silence

the campfire haunts me
a cage of small hours
surrounds me
calls out names
in the darkness
no one answers

a pack of coyotes
howl the moon
but disappear before
I can join the pack
and escape myself.

I Carry My Heart

I carry
my heart

fractured
and beating

inside of
my notebook

pieces on
each page

bleeding
in poems.

Uncharted

We kiss
below
a sea of pearls

two bodies
swimming
in constellations

buoyed by the moon
our hearts beat
like the tide

waves
crashing
between breath

a mist of fireflies
explodes in slivers
of dull light

eyes closed
we cast off
firm shores

sailing into
a midnight sea
of diamonds.

Night Full of Diamonds

Dipping
fingers

into sea
of stars

arms
outstretched

radiating
visage of desire

coiled galaxies
in your eyes

and me
here

fire kissed
and drowning

in the shadow
of trees.

You

She casts dreams
with her eyes
cerulean pools
spill stars
down her
cheeks
waves
falling on
the beach
a heart
echoing
in the emptiness.

Stars That Scatter The Night

Words flutter
from your lips
like birds

feathers
dancing softly
on my skin

a blue moon
floats
in your stare

and the stars
that scatter
the night

mirror my heart
that lays in pieces
on the floor.

My Muse

I dreamed
her fingers
knew my skin
and traced my soul

tacked my secrets
to the night sky
where they hung
on stars

and blew
in the wind
until they fell
and covered us

in truth.

I Kiss The Wind

You
keeper
of my heart
diamond
of the dark

I kiss
the wind
in hopes
it finds
your cheek
your eyes
your neck
your lips
all of you

I open
my arms
to the
emptiness
and hope
you fall
from a dream
into my embrace

You
keeper
of my heart
diamond
of the dark
with vacant hands
I cling
to the thought
of you.

Overcast

The sky
is heavy
with gloom

it seems
to rest
its burdens
on my back

there's no room
to move around
and I know
it's all eternal
there's no way
to escape

it'll always
be there
so I continue
moving along
like these clouds

and I know
all seconds
are temporary
and even now

they're gone.

Sunset

The sun
breaks over
the horizon

a million
shards
of light
thrown over
the field

falling
in shadows
that lay softly
across ponds
and stretch
thin over
rock palisades

the end of day
withers
like the once
vibrant petals
of a flower

withdrawing
in wounded
steps
to the shade
of trees

I'm left
standing here
alone
understanding
revolutions
composed
and eager.

Forest

I throw
my heart
onto the fire

it snaps
and pops

embers mix
with stars

flames dance
in a frenzy

like the thoughts
ignited in my head

the trees
stand tall

dropping shadows
that cover me

pinned down
by the darkest hours

you escape
my lips

in a whisper.

Day Dream

All things
are beautiful
in early
afternoon sun

the sky
is empty
of nocturnal
thoughts

drowned out
are the stars
glittering
the cosmos

like your eyes
shining in dreams.

The Descent

I write
my sadness
on the wings
of birds
burning
in the sun

scorched feathers
in flight
break apart

trails of soot
streak the sky
of blue

I watch
the ashes
catch the wind
and hope
in the sunlight
they find you
falling softly
upon your head
so you'll know

that I
was once there

with you.

At Night

You sleep
with a smile
on your lips
I still taste
the kisses
you left
on my own
earlier tonight
shortly before
you closed
your eyes
that looked
at me
with longing
and even
out of view
are still
so blue
and seem
to house
skies
as open
and vast
as those
above
unbridled
western
meadows
I awake

again
as cars
pass by
on the
dim street
outside the room
where we lay
braided
together
as slants
of light
pattern
the walls
and fall
across
our skin
in the
silent hum
of stillness
I smile
and watch
you dream.

Snow Moon

I want to tell you
that the moon
tonight
is beautiful

that it floats
over the city
like a cosmic pearl

I want to tell you
that it gleams
like your eyes

that it cuts
through clouds
like your smile
does my heart

I want to tell you
all of this
but it would
all be lies

for this moon
in all it's beauty
falls in all ways
when compared
to you.

Lost At Sea

Oh to swim
in the oceans
of your heart
deep and wild
pull me under
and drown me
in your arms
a bed of waves
rippling the night
stars falling
in your eyes.

Silence

I'm sitting here
in the cabin

on the edge
of night

the walls of seclusion
are sturdy

all are absent
but the astral bulbs

and they're
out of reach

like you.

Caffeine Dreams

I fell asleep
with a coffee
in my hand
a smile
on my face
and dreamt
of you
and me
together.

At Times

When the late
setting sun
removes light
from my room

and shadows
take root and grow
along the corners

where the flowers
that sit
on the table
are veiled
in dull radiance

it is then
that sadness pours
from the edges
of my heart
water
from a broken vase

petals of all colors
strewn about
and glistening
on the floor

I stand
in the damp

memory
with shards
in hand

ready
to puzzle
the pieces
back together
again.

Another Round

I swallow
my sadness
like a shot
of whiskey

drunk
on the
thought
of you.

Our Night

I want
to fall
into your
eyes

swim
down
to your
heart

come up
for air
and kiss
your soul

wrap you
in a shawl
stitched with
stellar thread

and lay
knotted together
on the shores
of a moonlit lake.

While You Dream

I'll be writing you
poems in the middle
of the night

as you sleep
eyelids covering
topaz souls
hair spread soft
across a pillow
in a bed I wish
to share

my words
will rise over
the horizon
on the rays
of morning

when you awake
and take in
the first glimpse
of day
when the sun
kisses your
eyes
think of me
my lips
on yours
always.

Below The Moon

The thought
of you
floods my head
and I'm drowning

struggling
to stay
above water

looking up
a shimmering
expanse

reminding me
of your eyes
looking back
at mine

but you're
not here
no one is.

Tonight

Stardust
falling from
a naked sky

I sketch
constellations
along your skin

a galaxy born
with each
kiss.

Winter

Even in
the coldest
nights
I am
warmed
by the
thought
of you

an embrace
of lips
fingers
tracing
scars
of lost
love

your hair
draped
like a sheet
over me

and I lay
falling into
your eyes.

She

You
my darling
beauty
are rays
of the sun

cast down
through
all of space
until you're
here

right here

in this
one
certain
point
in time

and we're
together
by the turn
of a stone

lay down
your love
across
my chest

and feel
my heart

that beats
for you

here

right here.

Patience

I've got
too much
time
for soul
searching

I'm all
thought out
at this
point

the only
thing
I have
left
is feeling.

Woodsman

Ax
chopping
loneliness

feeding
breath
of fire

flames
in pit
of kindling

your lips
your eyes
my heart

burning
twilight
ashes

float
in soft
breeze

settle
on shoulders
of morning.

The Highway

Iced over
with a thousand
years of sadness

the moon
avoids
my stare

my heart
a deer
in headlights

coyotes
crouched
on the edge

ready to pick
my bones
once again.

Moondog

Howling
every night
lost
or unfound

clouds
rolling
across
an ocean
of granite

celestial
pebbles
flicker
in heavenly
currents

swimming to
fog swept
shores
clinging
to dreams.

Remains

The sun recedes
like my hair line
my joints tighten
like the hangman's noose
before executing dreams
youthful shadows
collapse
after a long days work
and fall across
broken sidewalks
that lead nowhere
neighborhoods
boarded up
by lack of attention
with keys
still in the door
bones at a desk
ground to dust
by clocks
while curtains blow
in empty rooms
like white flags
surrendering
to the armies
of history.

Inishmor

I'm at
an Irish pub
in Colchester
alone
and waiting
for my burger
but the bartender
had my beer
waiting for me
when I walked in
every
so often
after kicking you
in the gut
for months
on end
the universe
relents
and sees to it
that you
have a remedy
to ease the pain.

Cloudburst

I went out
into that sad rain
alone

every misfortune
packed in my bag
tears falling
from the concrete sky

taking in the
vastness of life
I saw one
solitary bird
sitting motionless
on a limb

I stood for a bit
watching him
until his feathers
whispered the wind
and off he went

and I thought
to myself
I sure hope
he finds
whatever it is
he's looking for.

Interstellar

I want
to stand
down on
the shores
of the
old lake
with you
incandescent beams
spiral down
and lasso us
a luminous embrace
fingers entwined
I want your skin
touching mine
stars littering
the night
cosmic dust
falls from
our hair
and lips
your eyes
echo the galaxy
that has me
pulls me
to my knees.

Kill Time

Come,
kill time
with me
under a sky
so blue
and wide
it shines
like the Atlantic
in the early
light of dawn
kill time
with me
and sit
in the glow
of a campfire
that
burns
the dusk
like lanterns
igniting
the long
star dusted
hours
we spend
alive
killing time
together.

Constellation of Beings

I
want
my kisses
to cover
your
body
like a
silk sheet
soft
and damp
after
a summer
night
braided
together
by stars
eyes lit
by a lustrous
body of dust
reflecting
the cosmos
of bodies.

This Bed

You
dream of my heart
flower
of my earthen soul
blooming
in a forgotten
garden of weeds

you
stretching
heavenwards
towards
a desolate sun
hanging
in a soft sky

you
dream of my heart
flower
of my earthen soul
don't return
to dust
and clay
when stars
fall

leave your petals
and your thorns
for me

I want to hold
all of you
when night
descends upon
this bed
of brush
and tangled
vines.

Lincoln Woods

A filtered sun
splits through
tree tops

pours out
over mid morning
hours

there are
flowers here
along the trail

they are not
perfect
but that
is what contains
their beauty

dust
kicked free
from boots
clouds steps

untouched
and curving
towards corners
draped in shadows

forward.

About The Author:

Jake St. John spends his nights in a cabin on the edge of the woods. He is the author of several collections of poetry including Snow Moon (Holy & Intoxicated Publications, 2019) and Lost City Highway (A Jabber Publication, 2019). His poems have appeared in print and online journals around the world.

Night Full of Diamonds, is much more than a great collection of poems. It's an explorer's journal written by a man who understands, like so many others do, that it's a damn lonely feeling to be lost in life and left wandering around beneath the dark, long shadows that stretch out in the transition stage of yesterday into tomorrow. With each page turned, I had a desire to tie my bootlaces a bit tighter, strap on my own backpack, and join Jake St. John on the journey; punching holes deep into the shadows to expose on the other side, the sparkling pieces of pure grit, love, and beauty that lies hidden away from us all.

— Victor Clevenger, author of *A Wildflower In Blood*.